BROKEN BUT BEAUTIFUL

BlueRose ONE.com
Stories Matter
NewDelhi • London

BLUEROSE PUBLISHERS
India | U.K.

BlueRose ONE
Stories Matter
New Delhi • London

For permissions requests or inquiries regarding this publication,
please contact:

BLUEROSE PUBLISHERS
www.BlueRoseONE.com
info@bluerosepublishers.com
+91 8882 898 898
+4407342408967

ISBN: 978-93-7018-186-1

Typesetting: Pooja Sharma

First Edition: May 2025

In loving memory of my grandfather

Whose quiet wisdom and steady hands held my word together.

This is for you and your words echo through mine

About the author

Vanessa Shah is a poet who uses her art as an emotional outlet. Her poems are deeply personal and introspective, exploring a wide range of emotions, from pain and envy to happiness and love. The canvas becomes a metaphor for her own soul, bearing witness to her experiences and struggles. She is a poet who is not afraid to delve into the darker aspects of human nature but also finds beauty and hope in the midst of it all.

Overall, Vanessa Shah seems to be a passionate and talented poet who uses her art to connect with others and share her own experiences. Her poems offer a glimpse into her soul and invite readers to reflect on their own emotions and journeys. Vanessa Shah is a poet who dives deeper into the complexities of human emotions, particularly the experience of hurt. Her poems are introspective and thought-provoking, exploring the nuances of disappointment, betrayal, and the pain of lost connections.

Vanessa Shah seems to be a compassionate and insightful poet who uses her writing to explore the depths of the human experience. Her poems offer solace and understanding to those who have experienced hurt, while also challenging readers to consider their own role in creating and overcoming it.

Contents

Why me? 1
Death 2
Rollercoaster 3
If only 4
Woe 5
Broken 6
Pain 7
It's all lies 8
Crying in silence 9
The grass between my toes 10
Sick of surprises 12
The devil in fairyland 13
Unleashed rage 14
They don't see it how I do 15
Life 16
Positive changes 17
Except you 18
Darkness of the hurting souls 20
I'll never be better. 21
So, why you? 22
Butterfly 23
Intoxicated 24
Rising from the depth 26

Sacred memories........27
Hurt........28
The 16th may........29
Fragile yet unbreakable........30
My birthday........31
Brushstrokes on canvas........33
If I let my intrusive thoughts win........34
Silent battles........36
How to actually live........37
Live the moment........39
Stalker........41
One last time........43
Numb to the feeling........46
Somewhere between then and now........47
Cold hearted........48
Conflict with my emotions........49
Diverging destinies'........50
Misjudged beauty........52
The art of deception........54
Two souls adrift in separate storms........56
Moonlight murder........57
Silent echoes........58
Echoes of the abyss........60
Bruised........61
An angel's death........63
Broken by the bond created........64
A flutter of doubt........66

The silent scrivener 68
The brightest of the skies 70
The weaver's loom 71
Lost in the labyrinth of fate 72
Graces touch 73
Poisoned gloom 74
The Inner light 75
Loneliness filled by betrayed souls 76
How did I end up here? 77
The kingdom that I cannot claim 78
The Phoenix in ashes 80
Root of love in a forgotten land 81
Muffled whispers from the void 82
Victim's charade 84
The trapping spiral 85
A silent strain 86
The consumed darkness 87
Echoes in my mind 88

Why me?

From laughter to tears,
From road trips to empty rooms,
From sleepovers to lying alone on the floor,
How did we change?
Why did we stop telling our stories?
Why did we stop sending out fit checks to each other?
Why did we stop cringing on boy talks?
Why did we forget to laugh at our lame jokes?
Why was I the only one putting effort into making you happy?
Why do I give it all and receive nothing?
Why did you start to ghost me out of the blue?
Why did you leave me alone in this pain and misery?
Why did you leave me when I needed you the most?
Why me?
Why when you know I was broken inside?
I wish we would've checked out our bucket list
I wish you all the happiness in the world no matter where you are
I hope you remember those memories we built in the previous years
To those days when we felt alive when we were on the brink of death
When all our problems were forgotten, the 90s bangers blasted out our car.
Why did you choose me out of all the people you loved?

Death

It's not just a word but an emotion.

It's not just negativity but a form of freedom.

It's not just the opposite of life but also

a composition of purity and peace.

It's not just the removal from the first-world

but the entrance to the other world.

It's not just a different form of peace but also

unsatisfied revenge.

It's not just the pain but a sense of relief.

Rollercoaster

Breathe! Because you never know when this drowning amusement will turn into sorrow mixed with fear.

Breathe! Because this happy soul will soon be depressed and these fun-filled moments will turn into tears-filled rooms.

Breathe! Cause these giggles will turn into painful cries and muffled screams.

Breathe! Due to this large loop coming through your life will take a huge deflect.

If only

If only I could see those signs in front of me.
If only I could look through the thick glass.
If only I could breathe properly
If only I could be heard underwater
If only the stars would shine in front of me
If only the shadows stopped lying
If only the pictures could narrate the story
If only

Woe

Where were you when I needed a tight hug?
Where were you when the world got scarier?
Where were you when I started hurting?
Where were you when I needed a push to live?
Where were you when I fell apart?
Where were you when I needed the talk?
Where were you when life took a bad turn?
Where were you when I was broken?
You left me when I was deeply injured.
You left me when I needed you the most.
You disappeared.

Broken

If you loved me then why am I broken
If you cared then why am I broken
If you checked on me then why am I broken
If you were emotionally available then why am I broken
If you listened then why am I broken
If you saw me the way you said then why am I broken
If you were there for me then why am I broken
Because you never did anything you said you would
Because you left me in pieces
Because you left me hurting, drowning, breaking apart
You left me broken and only my bods could cure me
Only those were the real guardians
They were there when you left me broken

Pain

That fake smile
That screaming face
That unemotional hug
That aching soul
That hurting look
That shaken body language
Those painful tears
Those sorrow-filled eyes
That pain all along was love
That was what you wanted me to experience?
I wish I had known earlier
I wish I stayed away
I wish you consulted a therapist instead of putting me in pain too
I hope you healed
I wish you stopped hurting

It's all lies

Your eyes
Your smile
Your expressions
Your face
Your actions
Your conditions
Your situations
Your thoughts
Your opinions
That amazing fake identity
Those beautiful lies
Those fake promises
Those cover-up questions
I love the way you argue when you are wrong
I love the way you shower that irrelevant sarcasm
I love the way you present yourself when you're the problem
I love the way you look at me
I love the way you stare
I love the way you hate me
I love the way you care
I love the hatred-filled attention
I love the way you lie

Crying in silence

Restless body
Sweaty palms
Shaking hands
Swollen eyes
Irritated mood
Heavy breathes
Shivering and trembling legs
racing heartbeat and pulses
Rushing blood in veins
Voice powerless
Numb brain
All that for what
Those agitations
Those fake rumours
Those lies spread among
Those jealous smiles
Those vengeance seekers
That past
That boy
That friend
That lover
That heartbreak

The grass between my toes

Those parties

Those hangouts

Those happy hours

Those ball nights

Those drives

Those cries

Those off-road tours

Those restless hassles

Those workloads

Those paper piles

Those vacations

Those mountains

Those waterfalls

Those rainbows

Those rivers

Those oceans

Those bridges

Those boats

Those ships

Those things have no meaning unless you're with me

Those things are just fragments of life until you give a deep purpose to view them

Those things are nothing but part of life until you put a certain value on them

Those things are stars till you be the moon to outshine

Those things are life till you aren't afraid of death anymore

Those things are lifeless till you give them emotions

Those pretty things get it's priceless name based on how you describe them

Those things add value to your life when you see them the way you're supposed to

Sick of surprises

You surprise me with gifts
You surprise me with an attachment
You surprise me with love
You surprise me with care
You surprise me with Dior and Chanel
You surprise me with flowers and books
You surprise me with date nights
But they gradually changed
Now you surprise me with the distance
Now you surprise me with silence
Now you surprise me with emotional trauma
Now you surprise me with mental illness
Now you surprise me with unavailability
Now you surprise me with detachment
Now you surprise me with withered leaves
Now you surprise me with no respect
Now you Surprise me with abandonment
Now you surprise me with hate
Now you surprise me with lies

The devil in fairyland

I was war

They were peace

I was disaster

They were beauty

I was sorrow

They were happiness

I was death

They were life

I was destruction

They were my salvation

I was pain

They were cure

I was knife

They were bandages

I was tenebrous

They were illuminated

Unleashed rage

There is this rage in me that seeks vengeance
It wants to rip you apart
It wants to cause you pain
It wants to make you suffer every inch
It wants to tear you down
It wants to laugh at every downfall you experience
It wants to kill you
It wants to make you taste the cold serve of revenge
It wants to purely stab you
It wants to sprinkle salt on every deep wound you have
It wants to cut deep and trigger all your weak points
It just wants to see you suffer the way you make me feel lost and broken

They don't see it how I do

To the people who think that they have destroyed my world to see me grow better than ever

To the people who think that their rumours were enough to spoil my reputation

To the people who think that I can't live without them

To the people who always want to steal my personality from me

To the people who thought that being my friend and doing me wrong was a part of their personality

To the people who believe that they match my energy to be with me

To the people who assume that being my other half is a piece of cake

To the people who are convinced that distrusting me will send them fake popularity

To the people who think that disrupting my mental peace is a great achievement

To the people who think they gave their all to me knowing very well that I gave them more than I could have ever imagined

To the people who think that being something but fake to me is a life award

To the people who love destroying my happiness is enjoyment

To the people who think that loving me at first and ghosting with lame excuses is a Nobel prize. Just so you all know, I'm uprising from the pain and misery, be aware it may affect you.

Life

Life is a game

Some die, and some live

Some succeed some fail

Some buildup and some breakdown

Some love some hate

Some ace some lack

Some care some don't

Some are honest and some lie

Some play it well some don't

Some want to live it and some want to die

Some are given an extra companion but some are taken away

Some could play till the end some give up in the middle

Some take it positively some take it negatively

It's not just the game, but the experience of being a part of it.

It's about participation

It's about the guts to face the challenges

It's about the route, not the destination

It's about the journey, not the end

Some come and go

It's a part and parcel of this game called life

So accept and move on

Positive changes

From my darkest days to the summer mornings

From the coldest winters to warm summers

From the shady streets to fall trails

From snow storms to brain-freezing slushy attacks

From sick days to energy-blasting arcade visits

From phone calls to monthly hangouts

From sadness to happiness

From no moon nights to moonlight drives

From darkness to light

From pain to cure

From hurt to healed

Through the change

How did those five people change me?

How did those five people give me everything I needed and asked nothing in return?

I'm highly grateful for those souls.

I'm highly appreciative of knowing that I'm on your happiness list when all others kept me in the shadows and hatred.

Except you

I fell in love
With Italy
With Monaco
With Mexico
With the United Kingdom
With Japan
With Los Angeles
With Brooklyn
With New York
With Paris
With USA
With Mystic falls
With Costa Rica
With Satori
With Greece
With Bali
With Saudi
With the Middle East
With north
With south
With places
With tours
With food
With culture

With mansions
With books
Everything but you

Darkness of the hurting souls

The night in darkness and peace
The place where the light guides you through the path
The Place where all the anxiety, pressure and pain vanishes
The place where most are at peace
The place where calmness is devoured by sleep
The place where the stars shine brighter than ever
But somewhere deep down
People are drowning in that Darkness
People have destroyed the peace
People have devoured sleep through pain
People are found crying in thunderstorms which brings peace to most
People rethink their life decisions
People want to harm themselves under the cover of the night
People need to burst out of their pain
People pull out those hurtful memories and bottled-up emotions
People express the hidden pain after the fall of night
This moonlight which once gave peace to most now tries to soothe some
The dark clouds which are a sign of serenity to most now bring a sense of
terrible anguish to some Most find peace and some just suffer in pain

I'll never be better.

Could someone let them know that rating you out won't gain them anything

Could someone let them know that putting salt on my deep wounds won't make anyone jealous

Could someone let them know that if things should be secretive then saying it out loud won't certify them

Could someone let them know that people won't laugh at the lame jokes that they are making about me

Could someone let them know that if I don't want to share my reasons then they lack my trust

Could someone tell them if I don't like their company then don't force me to be with them manipulatively

Could someone let them know that a no means no

Could someone let them know that it's not always about them

Could someone let them know that I have a life unlike them

Could someone let them know that putting someone in trouble because of them doesn't mean you're the only one

Could someone let them know that it may ruin someone's mental health, reputation and state of mind

So, why you?

Why does it always have to be the ones we love?

Why does it always have to be betrayed by the one you care about?

Why does it always matter to me and not to them?

I accept that I made bad decisions but that doesn't mean you can do whatever you want with my soul.

It doesn't mean to rip my heart into shreds

It doesn't mean you have the right to kill those emotions

It doesn't mean that without working things out you can shut me out

It doesn't mean that I'm not hurt

It doesn't mean that you're the only one who I tried to love

It doesn't mean that it's you

But all I'm saying is why did you punish me for the things I was framed for?

Why did you hurt me for the rumours passed on?

Why did you shut me out for those misunderstandings?

Why?

Why did it have to be you?

Why did you have to hurt me?

Why did you not understand my circumstances?

Why did you feel untrusted when I did trust you blindly?

Why?

Why did you do it?

Butterfly

Sometimes I'm trapped
Sometimes I'm free in the wild
Sometimes I'm tortured and preserved
Sometimes I'm adored and taken care of
Sometimes I'm confined
Sometimes I'm hard to catch
Sometimes I make people sick
Sometimes I bring joy to people
Sometimes I'm ignored
Sometimes I'm being observed
Sometimes I'm viewed for my wings
Sometimes I'm viewed by the struggle
of transformation
Sometimes I'm on a flower bed
Sometimes I'm running in the stomach of the town lovers

Intoxicated

Down with that drug
Drugs of love and care
Drugs of pain and misery
Drug of detachment
Drug of connection
Drug of understanding
Drug of patience
Drug of silence
Drug of pure anguish
Drug of anger
Drug of understanding faith
Drug of emotions
Drug of hatred
Drug of torment
Drug of passion
Drug of affliction
Drug of exertion
Drugs of burning desires
Drug of strain
Drug of bitter trauma
Drug of pressure
Drug of happiness
Drug of a cold bloody fool
Drug of discomfort

Drug of loneliness

These will strike you better than nicotine,

morphine or cocaine

Rising from the depth

I'm comforted by the world of serenity
I'm rising above the stress which is weighing me down
I'm going to be okay
I've been through much worse
I'll make it this time
I'm proud of the past survived days
I'm proud of me
I'm rising from the pain that's driven me deep down
I have been there once before
I know I can do it
I have to keep fighting it
I can't give up now
I'm going to be fine
I'm a diamond
A little pressure will make me shine more
I accept people cannot change so I'll start the chain
I'm going to be okay
I'll make it

Sacred memories

Your warm hands
Your heartfelt words
Your soft speech
Your breathless kiss
Your engulfing grabs
Your heart-blazing gaze
Your warmth-filled hugs
Your sweet eyes
Your blazing spark
Your contradicting opinions
Your cozy arms
Your intense touch
Your comforting aura
Your adorable smile
Why?
Why do I miss it so much now, I
Didn't value it till you existed
But now that you don't
I feel the absence
Why did you leave me?
Why did you die before I could learn to express?
Why did you give up?
Why did you lose yourself for those filthy souls?
Just why?

Hurt

When are you hurt?
When do people leave?
When people ignore?
When people you love die?
When do those precious things break?
When sweet dreams turn into Nightmares?
No
It's When you think they cared
It's When you think they loved
It's When you think they were the one
It's When you think it had some emotions linked to it
It's When the meaning behind the sweet dreams and Nightmares
It's When you see the way the world sees it and you realize the difference that you only saw the good before it gives you the taste of hurt
It's When you believe they are doing it for you
It's When the efforts you think are made for you
It matters how you think
If you don't create that sense of attachment of emotions
Then, It will never hurt
If you grow out of the dilemma and unsee the way you saw them
If you didn't create that special bond in your heart
Hurt is intentional
If you train yourself for Ignorance
It may never come back

The 16th may

The day you saw me as something
The day you started to care
The day you started to love
The day you fell for me
The day you had those butterflies
The day you understood the meaning of love
The day you showed up on my front door
The day you talked to me for hours
The day you started lying about your past
The day you saw my eyes under the sun
The day it all started
The day that would've never occurred
The day you walked me home
The day you took me out
The day your hidden courage showed up
The day you couldn't risk
The day you started observing the details
The day you found happiness
The day you met me
The day you started expecting things
The day those small things started to matter
The day you accepted me
The day you saw something in me

Fragile yet unbreakable

I'm sensitive but not weak
I'm emotional but not frail
I see small details
I find my happiness in every small thing
I care too much but when I cut off I didn't even know you existed
I can be as soft as a flower
And as delicate as a bomb
Choose the right one
I can weep while showing you your place
I can sob while slapping you
You have to decide whether I'm your therapist or nemesis
I'm not for all to handle
I get mad but I can forgive
I can be furious but I can let go
But I'll never forget what you did to me
I'll keep that in mind till the grave
That pain you caused me may be forgiven but never forgotten
I try to hide the accumulated pain but it comes out anyway
I try to hush down the hurt in all ways but sometimes it overflows
The secrets I have kept in me
But the people left
The small gifts they've given me but the friends left
I can be soft but Dangerous when needed
It's all what I choose to show
So peaceful after they stop judging the mender and destroyer

My birthday

It's my birthday and You still hate me
You still ignore me
You still hang out with my Enemies
You still rage out at me
You still hate the way I was in your life
You still have those pictures to burn
You still won't talk
It's my birthday
My parents buy me gifts from Dior
I hope to share those with you
My parents get me a cake
I hope to cut it with you
My parents throw me a party
I hope you'll still come
My parents showered me with kind words
In hopes You would give me those heart-touching letters again
My parents give me a dress to wear on my special day
I hope you'll suggest me poses and click my photos
My parents record my happiness to watch me after 10 years
I hope you'll do the same It's my birthday
Yet again I'm lying on the floor thinking
What did I do wrong?
Where did I go wrong?
What did I do to cause you harm

What made you think I'm the monster

What made you think that I am the fake one

Yet again I'm lonely and empty

Yet again I am unable to reach how easily you could leave me right there when I needed you. It's my birthday.

I'm eating my emotions through that tasteless cake

I'm viewing my great skill of acting through the videos

I'm sitting in the veranda crying to the rain and hurting through the thunderstorm.

I can't go to bed with those unheard stories

I'm not the person who could let that go so easily

Brushstrokes on canvas

These canvases have endured all my emotions
Sometimes pain
Sometimes happiness
Sometimes envy
Sometimes revenge
Sometimes the hurt
Sometimes the lies
Sometimes those happy days
Sometimes that morning love
Sometimes that foolish self
These brushes felt my agony
They have cried on my canvas
They know my stories
They know my betrayals
They know who I am
They know about it all
But still managed to form trails
From snow storms on my empty canvas
They still manage to paint those lovesick people
No matter how much I try to let the past go
There's always a canvas waiting for me to depict a story on it

If I let my intrusive thoughts win

If I let them win
I'd be Harley Quinn
If I let them win
I'd be washing the blood stains
If I let them win
I'd be hiding it in the graveyard
If I let them win
I'd destroy many lives
If I let them win
I'd be framing it as a mere accident
If I let them win
The bickery would turn into a bloody war
If I let them win
I'd be breaking hearts
If I let them win
I'd be cold and emotionless
If I let them win
The red paint would be blood
If I let them win
I'd be living as the omega
If I let them win
I'd be taking control
If I let them win
People would think I'm a monster

If I let them win

I'd be hunted

If I let them win

It's all over for you all

Silent battles

Hey

What healed you?

What motivated you to just keep going?

What kept you from giving up?

What made you change your mindset?

Instead of these questions, I'm asked.

If I'm depressed or need help

If I tried to kill myself or not

If I broke the people I conversed with or not

If I destroyed someone by just being myself

It's all about perceptions and views

Today you may think that damn she escaped such tragic death

Tomorrow it may turn into damn how is she even alive?

To all the people who think mental health is not as important as physical health

Then, let me open your eyes

It's not that way

How to actually live

I'm surviving the rain
I'm surviving the heat
I'm surviving the cold
I'm surviving the mist
I'm surviving the fog
I'm surviving the snow
I'm just a sapling
But still, I survived the harsh weather of the world
Then, why can't you
You're stronger than me
You are 10 times the size of me
If I can survive all that pressure to be persistent and resilient all year
Then why do you try to fight and build yourself and let that one person destroy it completely
Then why don't you understand that if you spend all those years growing just to be eaten and crumpled down to pieces
I provide
You consume
Should be the case
What does it take
For a deep breath
To share those bottled emotions with someone you genuinely trust
To sit back and watch your favourite people succeed with your support
To just let things go

To value what you have

To stop cribbing over what left

To enjoy that beautiful sunset

Live the moment

To stop cringing on those hurtful times with them
To just feel happy and blessed the way you are
To stop crying about who gave more importance to someone else
To let it all go with the flow
We all have flaws
Some try to hide
Some can't
Some accept
Some coverup
Be in the broad daylight
With what you are and what you have
Never try to hide or fake it
It'll take you nowhere
Choose the bitter truth over a beautiful lie
Choose the harsh reality over demure delusions
Show what you are with all your flaws
Real people love you when
You're genuine and honest
Always remember to count on the people you care about and love
Because they know how perfect they match your energy
It takes one beautiful soul to know one
If you hesitate ever to talk about what's hurting then first find out what caused it.
Find out why

After you know the valid reasons take action accordingly and the best is to ignore

Surviving is the key to live

But if you enjoy while surviving then you actually lived

Stalker

He peaks
He comes by
He watches me
He stares
He loves
He adores
Every night by the porch
He delivers notes
He sends flowers
He gifts jewels
He paints me all-day
He has made me his hobby
He wipes my tears
He brings joy
He brings laughter
But he's a total Stranger
He calls
He cares
He keeps me safe
He's there, where no sun's ray falls
He's wild at heart
He's the different shades of cool
He has a different desire
He is my dark paradise

I feel observed

I feel watched

I feel thought about

I feel loved

One last time

I want that one last hug
I want that one last night with you
I want to watch that one last movie with you
I want that one last pep talk from you
I want that one last forehead kiss from you
I want to cry my eyes out one last time to you
I want to bid you goodbye
I want to keep you alive in every piece of me
I want to treat every affected organ
I want to see you one last time breathing
I want to see you one last time singing my birthday
I want to see you feeding me with your hands one last time
I want to breathe in your presence one last time
I want to feel your warm hands on my cheeks one last time
I want to sleep listening to you recite that prayer one last time
I want to feel your soul around me one last time
I want to bid you Farwell one last time
I want to give you that rose one last time
I want to have that special coffee with you one last time
I want to recreate that day one last time
I want to hold your hand one last time
I want to see you breathe on that ventilator one last time
I want to be there one last time
I want you to see my happiness one last time

I want you to see my success one last time

I want you to console me one last time

I want to see you one last time

I want you to wipe my tears one last time

I want you to see me jump round and around the house one last time

I want to ask you again that question one last time

I want you to come see me one last time

Poor heart

Oh! it burns

It kills

It destroys

It ventures

It ruptures

It breaks apart

It crushes

It melts down

It winds down

It is damaged

Just like the cheap gifts You gave

Just like the emotionless letters

Just like the unavailable unseen texts

The heart

It has the power to break another and be destroyed

It has the power to build again and kill

It carries these advantages and disadvantages

It holds all the love and pain

It swades along the good and bad

It crumbles and mends

It judges and cares

It hates and loves

It criticizes and praises

It ruins and fixes

It's all how you treat It

You get what you give

Numb to the feeling

There's a time period in life where it all felt numb
It's where you are just doing things for the sake of doing it
It's where the fireworks aren't as fun as they used to be
It's where the sweets turned into tasteless sand
It's where the soul is losing all the emotions
It's where the memories start to fade
It's where the hangouts don't excite the way they used to
It's where your favourite things turn into normal bullshit
It's where life loses It's spark
It's where none of it makes sense
It's where there are no highs or lows
It's just like the ventilator when the person's heart stops beating
It's where the sunset stops looking at you
It's When the moon cries at your state
It's When the wind doesn't feel like bothering you
It's When the sea wants to give you a tight hug
It's When the forests want you to keep bringing the spark in you
It's When the waterfalls want to bring back joy
It's When the alcohol seeks to forget and live that moment
The stage when all this pain converts into grieving silence
This is where self-harm enters
It's where you try to hurt yourself from physical pain but the catch is that the wounds keep growing deeper into the flesh
It's where the mental pain neutralizes the physical pain
The phase where it converts into physical tolerance because you mentally drained

Somewhere between then and now

I once wrote a dairy for 365 just to burn it later
I once bought a bouquet just to throw it out later
I once bought books just to tear it out later
I once loved a person just to be hurt later
I once bought a canvas just to ruin it later
I once bought ink to destroy it later
I once cared just to be ignored later
I once gave all my love out to the world just to be depressed later
I once overshared just to be the gossip later
I once broke down just to be called weak later
I once showed up just to be made fun of
I once cleaned just to be messy again
Why did anyone not see my efforts?
Am I a bad person?
Am I a bad Friend?
Am I a bad soul?
Then why do people treat me like trash?
Why am I prioritized over people when I give them the best?
Why am I always neglected by others?
Why am I broken?
Why do people not think before talking?
They treat me like shit and, then expect me to give them my world
Why do I give out love to every person and only receive nothing but hate in return?

Cold hearted

Uncomfortable gaze

Unheard stories

Ice cold body

Frozen heart

Sarcastic laugh

Tiny smirk

Killer personality

Murderous nature

Stalker love

Electrical aura

Cold-blooded veins

I have always seen you jolly till you upgraded from the past

Where did the fun adventures wild ambitious soul disappear?

Why did you shut people out and start acting upon rumours and bullies?

Why did you become the one picking fights with people

But I know somewhere deep down there is a sweet child inside waiting to come out to the world

But I know deep down you care and the guilt hurts

I know that it's not easy

When everyone argued about losing something or the other

You asked if they lost everything at once

I know that sweet loving part of you has been suppressed by the pain and anguish

Conflict with my emotions

There's is this conflict within my emotions
One day it's drowning in the depth of darkness
It's calling for help
It's buried down in the vertical extent of the Sahara
It's shaking inward parts of the ocean
And one day it yelps for happiness
It calls out the child from the dark
It brings out the best in me
It shows up at my door unnoticed for a prom night
It uplifts me like a guiding light
It finds cure
It gives peace
But sometimes it turns into a deep greed
It changes its colours to a burning desire
It feels like a tangled mess within
It pushed me to lands of confusion and misery
It makes me act shameless, nonsense and I'm embarrassed
It's not just that
Sometimes it overflows exposing the inner contentment
It shows the hidden corners
It unfolds the covers to reveal the raw view
It unveils the tales of the bottled and deeply suppressed agony
It feels like manipulative black magic
It feels like unheard wants
It feels all too over the top

Diverging destinies'

I was the ocean
You wanted the rivers
I was the moon
You wanted to chase the stars
I was the canvas
You wanted the brushes
I was the flower
You wanted the leaves
I was the diamond
You wanted the alloys
I was the book
You wanted pages
I was the ink
You wanted the pen
I was the reality
You wanted the dream
I was the cure
You wanted the syringe
I was the bookmark
You wanted the ribbon
I was the house
You wanted the decor
I was the soul
You wanted the body

I was the road
You wanted the car
I was the light
You wanted the torch

Misjudged beauty

rage is like a forest fire
sweetheart is like grape vines
personality is like the smell of success
nature is like the beautiful sunsets
skills is like the titian aurm
soul is like the valley of dandelions
the body is like burgundy colour
gaze is like the shades of black
Eyes are like pools of honey under the sun
Nails are like the expensive marble flooring
Jealousy like the cheap gifts
Fever like global warming
Obsession like spectrophillia
Hair like the fine threads of silk
Curves like the hill roads
Yet they only see the false rumours
Fake description
Tiny faults
Mistakes never committed
False accusations
And blackmailed proof
Hidden Depths,
Shallow Perceptions
Golden Heart

Tarnished View

Silk and Marble

Muddied Lens

A Tapestry Unraveled

A Misguided Gaze

Beneath the Surface is

A World Unknown

The art of deception

You knew it all along
You said nothing
You let me break
You let them burn me down
You saw me drown
You let them kill
You kept their secret
All along
You knew it was all planned
You knew it was going to put me down
You still played along
As if its nothing
You help them put me at my worst
You were there in their win
You made it all seem a coincidence
You made false rumors
You were the hidden one
You were the blind side
You were with them all along
You made it seem like a game
Until it destroyed me
You knew that it was harming
Yet you kept going
You were the black eye

You were the alibi

You knew all along

You burried me deep down

You stabbed all my wounds

You restricted my words

It's was you behind the name

You knew all along

A mind's tapestry

I'm high

With the drug called life

Where the oxygen makes me drunk

And the blackmailed proof of the day shines

Where the fireworks collide with the twilight sky and the manipulation of darkness brings light

Where memories creep within my soul

And the guilt trip outshines the gold

Where ocean meets the sun after dawn

And the guiding light pushed through thoughts

Where the sunsets collide with smoke in the redwood forest and the beauty of rain pull me back to reality

Where the smell of home-cooked food brings joy and happiness of letting them go brushes past my lingering soul

Where all myths turn into beautiful woven truth and the gut lies sometimes to ignore those sirens

Where the pebbles ripple through the still water lake and the evocation floats by

Where the evening tea turns into red wine and finding all ways to lose my mind

It's all in my head but I wish to be heard once

It's all fragments of my imagination but I wish to be seen once

Here I am Where reality fades and my imagination reigns

Two souls adrift in separate storms

Her coffee kept getting cold as she was waiting for him to miss her

whereas his cigarettes were running out one after the other to forget her

Her with her bestfriend shed tears of hope that he will remember her

whereas his car ate fuel as he tried to wipe her from his memories with his buddy

Her nights turned sleepless in hopes of have him back

whereas his nights spent gaming and finding all ways to lose her connection

Her heart ached in silence whereas his mind clouded with smoke

She held in silence hoping he would reach out

whereas he numbed the doubt with smoke

Both drowning in their own world neither reaching out

The distance between them grew wider and wider with every sip and puff

She wished for a call ,a sign ,a spark but

he sat in silence and shadows lost in the Dark

The city lights reflected in her tear-filled eyes as she watched the world pass by lost in lonely sighs

whereas He's in the smoky haze in the captive of the night, Searching for solace and completely lost in the fading light.

Moonlight murder

Nights where canvas shadows creep
A silent stage where secrets sleep
Beneath its cloak there's darkness deep
Where crimes unfold the secrets keep
A moonlit sky of a chilling sight
As murder stalks in the fading light
A twisted dance of wrong and right
A chilling scene what a dreadful plight
The city sleeps like a slumbering beast
A killer's heart growing the wicked feast
A life extinguished and a soul released
The night descends in the solemn hour
As shadows lengthen through losing power
A haunting memory of a tragic shower
Night's cloak descends in a velvet shroud
Where shadows dance and the secrets crowd
A canvas painted with inky hues
Where twisted plots and crimes ensue
Beneath the moon's indifferent eye
A silent stage where shadows die
A chilling wind whispers through the night
As darkness claims a soul's last light
The air grows thick with fear and dread
As secrets rise from the silent dead
A haunting echo and a mournful sigh
As night descends and truth draws nigh

Silent echoes

A gallery of silences,
Unspoken and deep
A haunting hush where memories creep.
The silent shock like a picture's ghost
A farewell's echo is a painful cost.
The stifled breath
a secret's weight
A year's reflection
a mournful fate
The missed chance,
a word left unsaid
A love betrayed
a trust misled
A fleeting scent
a phantom's trace
A mournful melody
a haunting space
The empty solace
a helping hand
A forgotten past across the land
A vacant stare
A picture's ghost
a memory's snare
A lingering sigh

A secret seen
a tearful eye
A year's stark mark
a missed reply
A broken trust is a lover's lie
A fleeting scent
A selfless act
a lonely plea
A faded dream like a word unspoken
A heart now broken is a spirit broken

Storm-Bound Secrets

Dark clouds gather over the tempestuous sea
A ship adrift long lost and weary
A private island shrouded in night
A siren's song what a dangerous sight
Moonlit caves where all the shadows reside
and all Deadly sins with a treacherous tide
A heart of darkness and a soul's demise
A storm-bound secret is a tragic prize
The wind howls while the waves crash and roar
A shipwrecked soul forevermore
A siren's call is a haunting plea
A prisoner of darkness long lost at sea.
Storm-Bound Secrets
Dark clouds gather in the tempestuous sea.
A ship adrift long lost and weary

Bruised

Beneath a mask of porcelain grace
A storm rages
An unseen disgrace
Her eyes
once bright
now shadowed and deep
Hide secrets dark
where sorrow sleeps
A fragile flower
battered and bruised
Her spirit shattered
Her hope diffused
Yet, still she blooms
A sight to behold
A canvas painted in silver and gold.
Her smile
A mask
A fleeting disguise
A brittle shield against cruel skies
Her laughter and whisper
A hollow sound beneath
Lost in the echoes
A paradox she is
A mystery untold

A beauty marred

A heart grown cold

For in her depths

A darkness resides

A haunting sorrow that forever abides

An angel's death

Faded Wings there is a celestial soul which was once pure and bright
Now, it fades to dusk what a mournful sight
An angel's wings were once strong and bold
Now droop and wither with every frail in cold
A heart once filled with love divine
Now aches with sorrow and a mournful sign
A spirit pure now lost in lone
A tragic tale with a sombre tone
A fallen star and broken dream
A fading hope with a fleeting gleam
The angel weeps after a silent tear
As death approaches and draws near
No solace found and no peace in sight
What a tragic end to a mournful night
The angel's spirit takes its flight
Leaving darkness to a haunting sight

Broken by the bond created

A Fractured Heart

Once a heart was so pure and bright
Yearned for love with all its might
She gave her all without a doubt
A love so deep that no words could spout
A soul once pure is now shattered and torn
A love once bright is now withered and worn
She gave her all, her heart, mind, and soul
But met with disdain to a heavy toll
For him, she'd climb the highest peak
But fate's cruel hand had a bitter twist
Her love rejected like a painful mist
Insults like sharp daggers pierced her core
A love once cherished now evermore
A fight ensued for a desperate plea
To mend the bond to set spirits free
But understanding through
And once a guiding light
Faded away lost and now dimmed by shadows shrouded in night
His selfish needs were a heavy load
In her heart, now weary and on life's road
She yearns to let go and break free from pain
A shattered soul adrift in the rain
No longer bound by love's cruel art

She'll heal her wounds with a brand-new start
A Heart Adrift, A desperate plea, A futile fight
To mend the broken and to restore the light
But understanding is a precious art
That had faded away and torn apart
He sought solace with a selfish plea
Ignoring her pain and her agony through
A love once shared
It is now lost and gone
A heart adrift forever alone

A flutter of doubt

I flutter near in a fragile sight
A heart unsure but a trembling flight
He fills my dreams like a radiant sun
But darkness lingers for the battles won
I crave his touch and his whispered praise
But doubt's cold hand obscures my gaze
I yearn for love and a gentle kiss
Yet fear rejection with a painful abyss
He sees my worth and the beauty of rare
But I perceive flaws of a burden to bear
I long to bloom as a vibrant flower
But insecurities choke hour by hour
He offers solace with a tender hand
But I push him away with a troubled land
I crave his love with a burning desire
But self-doubt's flames consume my fire
Oh, to be loved like a cherished sight
But first I must find my own light
To break the chains of self-disdain
And embrace the love I truly gain
A flutter in my chest is a nervous fight
A heart unsure lost in the night
He fills my dreams through a vision of bright
But self-doubt clouds my hopeful sight

A touch of warmth in a moment of bliss
Afraid to hope and afraid to miss.
But I perceive flaws as a burden to bear
I long to bloom carefree and fair
But insecurities bind me unaware
I crave his love like a burning desire
But self-doubt's flames stifle my fire
Oh, to be loved of my heart's desire
But first I must learn to admi

The silent scrivener

The Dual Existence of
A mind adrift and a soul confined
In realms of ink finds a peace entwined
A scholar's guise wears a mask of lore
A hidden depth forevermore
A yearning heart that seeks skies above
To feel the breeze of boundless love
To wander free is a spirit light
Escaping shadows into the night
A paradox of a curious sight
A lazy soul yet burning bright
A hidden talent has a secret grace
A silent strength of a hidden pace
A dreamer's world is a waking dream
A hidden hope of a cherished scheme
A quiet mind of a restless heart
A dual existence is torn apart
Bound by Brooks is a captive mind
A world of words is a solace kind
A dreamer lost in pages deep
A secret hope for a wish to keep
A scholar's guise a mask well-worn
A hidden spark is a talent born
A lazy soul with a languid pace

A fleeting glance is a vacant space

Yearning for fields is the open sky

A chance to roam to wonder why

A fleeting thought of a wistful sigh

A longing heart is a reason why

A paradox of a puzzling sight

A hidden depth of a blinding light

A silent scribe resides in a secret heart

A hidden dream and a work of art

The brightest of the skies

Oh, to be loved with a tender sight
A heart so pure and a soul so bright
Through stormy seas and skies of grey
Your spirit shines like a hopeful ray
In darkest hours when hope is lost
Love's gentle hand is my precious cost
It's in the touch, the word, the sigh
A love that lifts you to the sky
So, I let my heart forever mend
And let love's warmth forever lend
For in this world vast
True love's embrace is a precious tide
Drowning in the Pool of Love
Submerged in depths of hearts aflame
A captive soul written in a lover's name
The waters rise with a sweet despair
As love consumes beyond compare
A drowning heart in oceans deep is
Yearning for love is just like a promise to keep
The currents pull like a passionate tide
A soul entwined through a lover's guide
Oh, to escape this love's embrace
To find a respite in a peaceful space
But for now, I'll sink and yield
In the prison of love's battlefield

The weaver's loom

A canvas stretched, a mind laid bare,
A poet's soul, beyond compare.
With words as threads, a tapestry they weave,
A masterpiece, emotions they believe.
A rhythm's beat, a rhyme's sweet sound,
A painted picture, on hallowed ground.
A single verse, a universe untold,
A magic touch, a story bold.
From darkest depths to heavens high,
A poet's gaze, that pierces the sky.
They capture dreams, in ink and light,
And paint the world, with all their might.
So let us praise, the poet's art,
A gift divine, a work of heart.
For in their words, we find our own,
A piece of soul, forever known.

Lost in the labyrinth of fate

What if today's the final scene

What if the curtain falls and my life is unseen?

What if the path I chose with care

Now leads to shadows of dark despair?

What if my daggered heart ached just to end up like a wounded soul,

What if the heavy burden is in-depth and hard to whole?

What if these echoes of decisions made in past are now becoming the haunting wind and chilling blast

Will fate's cold hand on my life now claim the tragic end with my mournful name?

Or will a flicker of hope endure me with a ray of chance to heal and find a future pure?

The unknown looms wind me in a mystery deep with the fateful future veiled in my troubled sleep.

Yet, in the darkness, I'll still strive

To find the strength to stay alive

What if it's all over today

What if all that happened in the end to kill every remaining part of me

What if the choices I made will end up stabbing me in the end

Graces touch

I cried oceans for you
but you never let me drown
The tears I wept like boundless sea
but with a mournful soul adrift and free
I yearned for solace like the gentle hand
you gave to guide me through this barren land
You stood beside me like a steadfast guide
A ray of bright like to my darkest tide
You did not let my spirit drown
But lifted me to serenity and peace.
Your love is like a raft of saving grace
You painted hope on sorrow's face
I cried for you with an endless pour
But you returned and healed my core

Poisoned gloom

The storm raged within the tempest of soul,
Two jagged edges where the form of love is taking its toll.
A dance of defiance with passion so fierce,
Where tenderness whispered yet danger was near.
He then shadows brooding through a heart full of night,
She the flame burning defiant just like a fierce light.
They clashed and they clung
A dangerous game then begun
A love built on ashes whispering each other's name.
She the cage of thorns, he the bird longing to fly,
Yet bound by the chains of this love reaching for the sky.
She then tempest raging, a soul forever torn,
He the fragile flower by the fierce winds forlorn.
The beauty was fleeting
In a fragile fleeting grace,
Replaced by the poison, the pain on his face.
He wounded beast lost in the shadows' embrace,
She withered and broken, finding no solace.
In the end, the darkness consumed them both
A love that devoured leading to a suffocating oath.
He, lost in the abyss though a soul forever damned,
He was broken and shattered, a love that left him maimed.

The Inner light

The Butterfly is a fleeting grace
Unconscious of her sweet face
With wings of hues like a vibrant show
She dances unaware of the awe below
The world enraptured gazes on her
A masterpiece drawn beneath the dawn
Her fragile form entwined with a fleeting sight
A symbol pure in beauty's light
And in her flight resides a lesson that constantly lies
For hearts that yearn beneath the skies
For friendship's love burns tender bloom
May often hide within life's gloom
The pain we bear of a heavyweight
May dim the joy and seal our fate
But deep inside a spark remains
Of love's soft glow that gently reigns
Like the Butterfly, we may not see
The beauty born within us free
But others gaze with eyes so bright
And cherish us with all their might
So let us rise above the pain
And find the grace that love sustains

Loneliness filled by betrayed souls

Betrayed by bonds
a heart is now torn,
A trust once held is now frail and worn.
A friendship's flame
which once burned bright,
Now flickers dimly lost in the night.
I gave my all without a doubt,
Prioritizing you leaving others out.
I shielded you from life's harsh blows,
But now I stand alone where heartache grows.
They chose the new fleeting gleam,
Ignoring the bond is a forgotten dream.
While I remained steadfast and true,
Their loyalty wavered a different hue.
The pain cuts deep like a wound untold,
A friendship's promise now grows cold.
Yet, I'll rise above with strength renewed and
Learning the lesson in solitude.

How did I end up here?

The world is a huge stage where shadows dance of joy and grief lingering in a bittersweet trance.

The innocent weep, the wicked rejoice
A cruel discord and a discordant voice
The hungry plead while wealth overflows
The weak succumb as the tyrant grows
A tapestry torn out of hope and despair
A heavy heart with a soul beyond repair
How did I end up Here, in search of peace I only found things above and worse than pain.

I expected more to this world than war and death.

The kingdom that I cannot claim

The world is the crown I cannot claim,
A kingdom so vast I'm privileged to hear my whispered name
To offer you a feeling called love so grand
But shattered shards lie in this sand
My heart is a suffocating vessel cracked and torn
By echoes of love forlorn
The meaning has been lost like a fading gleam
A hollow space is just my forgotten dream
Yet, you ignite a strange desire
Worship born of primal fire
You make me feel like sacred ground with each step you take
A path I'd follow for goodness sake
And in this twisted broken grace
I have found love in this strange space
A love that kills and a love that blinds
Where convenience reigns no conscience binds
You are the treasure I can never tame
My heart is a rusted cage
Where love lies buried in the redwood book's forgotten page
You walk like a god among the throng,
Your symphony of grace is the whispered song ringing restless in my ears
You worship me not for the soul I hold
But for the power you command and the stories I tell
My love is a twisted venomous bloom

Just as a parasite feeding on his borrowed gloom
I crave the thrill of the hunt, the kill
To purge the world of all that might spill
For your eyes, I see a kindred spirit
A reflection of the darkness I inherit
A love born not of tenderness and grace
But of destruction not leaving my trace
You bring the spark back to my dead soul And cold eyes

The Phoenix in ashes

A cage of shadows where my heart resides,
Where suppressed pain eternally abides.
Pressure mounts constantly with a heavyweight,
Stress and anxiety is my suffocating fate.
The past comes in like a ghost, returning to haunt my nights,
With memories sharp in the void, chilled and icy.
Overthinking's grip leaves relentless scars on me,
Sleepless nights where my stories are often told.
Two minutes of brightness is a fleeting, fragile gleam,
Followed by torment, a soul-crushing stream.
A week of anguish, unbearable and deep,
Ungrateful agony, where my sorrows seep.
Will this ever cease, this endless, dark descent?
Or will this affliction forever be my tent?
Will I recover, find solace and release?
Or will it consume me, bring my spirit to its knees?
Will I emerge the same, after this cruel embrace?
Or will I be forever changed, leaving no trace
Of the person I once was, vibrant and so free,
Lost in these shadows, eternally

Root of love in a forgotten land

He fortress of my heart but it lonely to keep
Where walls rose high and secrets slumbered deep
A solitary reign shone in the shadows like a guarded throne
Where love's soft touch was ever overthrown
But then you came in just like a whisper on the breeze
A melody that calmed my troubled seas
You scaled the walls with a gentle and quiet grace
And found a haven in this lonely space
You settled deep within the soul's embrace
A tender root in this forgotten place
And with your presence and warmth began to bloom
Dispelling shadows I began chasing the distant gloom
The fortress crumbled down and the walls began to fall
As love's sweet surrender answered freedom's call
And in your arms a newfound peace I see
Where love resides eternally
With your love grace and serenity, my soul longing has ended and my heart beats at ease

Muffled whispers from the void

The world has me crushing its weight,
shadows suffocating my soul, deep down I fight battles with my demons within.
Obeying the law is my only escape.
A void that bares me is uncanny and vast,
alluring its madness, whispers of the unheard,
too much for one soul to bear in the eternity
Grief, burden, pain, and agony,
clustered in a small mind.
Selfishness, a shield against my hurt,
numbing the abyss,
or physical drainage,
a release from the maddening vessel is the only way.
The heart is my prisoner of despair,
yearning for solace and a discordant moment of peace,
in this world of shadows and pain.
I seek forgiveness and peace.
The world's weight crushes me,
shadows suffocate my soul,
Deep down I fight battles
with demons within.
Obeying the law is my only escape.
A void bares itself, uncanny and vast,
alluring madness whispers,

unheard, in eternity,
too much for one soul to bear.
Grief, burden, pain, and agony,
clustered in my small mind.
Selfishness, a shield against the hurt,
numbing the abyss,
or physical drainage,
a release from this maddening vessel.
My heart, a prisoner of despair,
yearning for solace,
a discordant moment of peace,
in this world of shadows and pain.
I seek forgiveness and peace.

Victim's charade

In Mirror's Maze, I find her Fractured Soul
A twisted game, a self-inflicted toll.
She is a master of the art,
Of feigning wounds, a broken and bleeding heart.
She craves the gaze, the pity, the despair,
A drama staged, a mask beyond compare.
My role was just to comfort her embrace,
Ignoring the truth is a self-destructive race.
She sows the seeds of chaos, then she weeps and weeps
A crocodile's tears, while others softly sleep.
Her actions masked were just a calculated game,
To shift the blame, to fan the flames.
She twists the knife, then cries out in distress,
A wounded soul, a fabricated mess.
The world believes, her act is a masterpiece,
A tragic hero lost in loneliness.
But deep inside, a void they cannot fill,
A hunger for control, a thirst to kill.
The empathy she craves, she could never feel,
A hollow shell, a wound that won't heal.
So let her play, her self-destructive game,
A tragic farce, a whispered in a haunting name.
For, in the end, her mask will surely fall,
And truth will rise, exposing one and all.

The trapping spiral

I bleep through this loop of life,
The loop spins, a dizzying blur,
Childhood's scars, forever stir.
Each turn, a soul bleeds slowly,
A fragile mind, a desperate flow.
The smile, a mask, a crafted facade,
Hiding cracks, a heart eroded.
Then, pain erupts, a searing wave,
Washing clean the brave facade.
Trust, a thread, now frayed and torn,
Detachment's grip, a soul forlorn.
ADHD's chaos, OCD's tight hold,
A mind adrift, a story untold.
Snakes encircle, judgment's sting,
Teachers' scorn, is a heavy thing.
Parents' peaks, a distant climb,
Shattered dreams, wasted time.
The future looms, a shadow's blight,
A path unknown, where sorrows bite.
Strength wanes, hope a fading gleam,
Lost in echoes of a forgotten dream.

A silent strain

I was always mature for my age,
A quiet soul on a chaotic stage.
I understood everyone's pain,
Yet no one saw my silent strain.
I was just a child, forced to be grown,
Carrying burdens I should've never known.
A heart that ached with empathy's sting,
While my own wounds went unhealed, unspoken.
I yearned for laughter, for carefree days,
But responsibilities cast a sombre haze.
I built a wall around my fragile soul,
To shield my pain from the world's cold.
But even walls have cracks, and tears find ways,
To trickle through in the lonely hours.
I longed for someone to understand,
To see the child within, to reach out a hand.

The consumed darkness

The darkness consumes me whole,
Makes me wonder, losing control.
Is the light a cruel deceit,
Or is the shadow's embrace, bittersweet?
With scars that have stained me completely,
Will I ever recover, eternally?
Just a survivor, or a soul decayed,
By the darkness, forever swayed?
The devil crawls, a serpent's guide,
Through the shadows, where my demons reside.
He has sinned, a soul forever stained,
Yet a purity within remained.
Brought me to light, a vision so grand,
But the price of his grace, I couldn't withstand.
Heartly destroyed, by his twisted game,
Trapped in this darkness, forever the same.

Echoes in my mind

You don't need to remind me,
The words hang heavy to plea.
A love declared, yet shadowed deep,
Where doubts and secrets softly sleep.
Want to put it all behind me, but, baby,
A fragile hope, a whispered maybe.
The past it lingers, a haunting trace,
A familiar ache, in time and space.
I see her in the back of my mind,
A phantom figure, intertwined.
All the time, a constant sting,
A melody the shadows sing.
Feels like a fever, like I'm burning alive,
Emotions blaze, where truths survive.
A burning question is my silent plea,
Is this real, or just for me?
Like a sign, a cryptic clue,
Did I cross the line, with me and you?
A boundary blurred, a heart in doubt,
Where love and longing wander about.
You say no one knows you so well,
But do you know yourself, I can't quite tell.
A veil of mystery, a hidden face,
In this tangled dance, we lose our place.

The echoes linger, a haunting strain,
A love that's whispered, through sun and rain.
A wildflower's struggle, to bloom and grow,
In the tangled garden, where shadows flow.